Discovering Christ's Presence
A Study Guide to Presence

R. Thomas Ashbrook

Unless otherwise noted, scripture is taken from the NEW AMERICAN STANDARD BIBLE Copyright © 1960, 1962, 1963, 1968, 1971, 1972, 1973, 1975, 1977, 1995, by the Lockman Foundation.

Readers should be aware that Internet Web sites offered as citations and/or sources for further information may have changed or disappeared between the time this was written and when it is read.

Library of Congress Cataloguing-in-Publication Data

Ashbrook, R. Thomas

Presence: What if Jesus Were Really Here? / R. Thomas Ashbrook

Library of Congress Control Number: 2015902493

    ISBN: 978-0-9916368-3-9

1.   Spiritual Formation. 2. Christian Fiction. 3. Inspiration
Printed in the United States of America

    First Edition

TABLE OF CONTENTS

Introduction

Of course, you know that Jesus lives Present with you. This Study Guide is provided to help you experience that wonderful reality more fully! Life with God vibrates with adventure, particularly because of its mystery and eternal nature. While the Holy Spirit gives us the capacity to know the Father, Son, and Holy Spirit, experientially, living fully in that capacity has to be developed; we have to learn to walk in the light; it's spiritual light which often feels like darkness to our natural minds. May the Holy Spirit become your teacher and your capacity expander as you explore deeper intimacy with Him in the following pages.

It's one thing to read a story, to connect with its characters, relate personally or not, and hopefully to be encouraged, taught, and even entertained. It is quite another thing to hear God speaking personally in the midst of the story line, and still harder to keep track of what God might want us to do with those inner stirrings of the Holy Spirit. This Study Guide is provided as a companion to *Presence* to help you dialogue with God in the midst of the story and ultimately experience more of Jesus—Present. While the story of Jesus' Presence to Jim, Lillian, and Barry was fictional, His Presence to you is certainly not! The Father, the Son, and the Holy Spirit are right here, closer than your breath, loving you and waiting to make their Presence known. They long to take the very best of the discoveries of our story characters and make them experiential realities for you. If you haven't already, you might want to simply read *Presence* through and simply enjoy the story. Then explore the study guide to invite God to touch you more deeply.

Discovering Christ's Presence provides a labyrinth, something like a computer game, to facilitate your reading and reflection. Within the maze of God's mysterious love you will encounter the Persons of the Trinity and your own heart. You'll be invited to make choices based on your discernment, and receive the power of the Holy Spirit as you explore more deeply. This discovery is best experienced with other explorers who can help you in challenging places and shed additional light into dark corners.

Please take note the Introductory and Follow-up Retreat formats in Appendix B. Especially if you are using study guide in a group, an introductory retreat could significantly deepen both the personal and group experience of the ongoing, chapter by chapter reflection and discussion. Therefore, the following format would be ideal process for use of *Discovering Christ's Presence.*

> **Read *Presence***
> **Introductory Retreat**
> **Regular meetings working through the study guide**
> **Follow-up Retreat**

Discovering Christ's Presence will guide your adventure in three distinct movements.

1. **Personal Study and Reflection** provides an opportunity to stop and listen to your own heart and to the Holy Spirit in the midst of your reading and to "notice." You'll want to notice the context in which you are reading that day. What has God been up to? Why this chapter today? What's the connection? Then

you'll want to notice what gets your attention in the story. What moved you, either positively or negatively and why? When did your brow wrinkle with skepticism or your heart leap in anticipation? Notice what Jesus seems to be doing, IN YOU. Use the questions in this section to explore your reactions to the events of the chapter. Use the Scripture passage to gain another perspective and notice what God says to you personally. Take notes in the Journal section to help you recall your experiences later, and to share them.

2. **The Spiritual Exercise** opens a three-dimensional viewer into your own story with Jesus. Taking the pathway of a scriptural text related to the theme of the chapter, you can let the Holy Spirit guide your imagination as you enter into the biblical story. Allow Jesus to shed new light upon your journey with Him. In the privacy of your own heart, you can sense, feel, listen, speak, wait – and let Jesus love you. Become attentive to His Presence through a challenge or an insight, or maybe through a holy silence where His still small whisper speaks inaudibly to your heart. Try to spend at least a half hour in the Spiritual Exercise, listening with anticipation. Again, journal your experience.

3. **Group Discussion and Reflection** helps you discern Jesus' Presence with more clarity. Hopefully, you will encounter enough mystery in the preceding two movements that you will want to talk to someone about it, to explore the grandeur of God's love for you with others who also long to know His Presence. In a community of fellow followers of Jesus, you can further explore your own journey, in the light that God may be giving to others, and ask with Jim, Lillian, and

Barry, "What's next?" Your prayers together receive the power to live into your discoveries.

So, whether you use this Study Guide simply to glean more from *Presence*, as a personal devotional guide, or for a small group discussion, ask Jesus to make His Presence known to you in a transforming way. With your cooperation, you and those around you are in for an adventure! He's Present!

A Note to Small Group Leaders: What a wonderful privilege to be asked to guide a group of Christ's beloved into a deeper exploration of His Presence. Of course you wouldn't be leading this group unless you possess the same desire for personal exploration. To help facilitate your role as a guide and fellow explorer, I'd like to offer a few suggestions.

1. First, don't over-lead. While some small group experiences need a leader who must guide the participants through scriptural investigation or provide questions which will prompt deeper investigation of a topic, this small group experience is intended to be a DISCOVERY – a personal discovery and interaction with the Presence of Jesus. Jesus doesn't want to force Himself on the participants, and neither should you. Your role in this discovery is to help provide a safe place for exploration, where Jesus sets the pace and reveals what only He knows needs revealing.

2. The group needs you to watch the time, see that everyone has an opportunity to contribute without being put on the spot.

3. They need you to participate with your own explorations, not as an expert but a fellow follower of Jesus.

4. They need you to remind them of the ground rules of confidentiality, abstinence from advice-giving and judgment. We're all on the journey of discovery. While some may have been at it longer than others, when

compared with the infinite mystery of God, we're all beginners.

Here's an approximate time breakdown for a Group Discussion and Reflection of two hours that can help the participants focus on the real deal – Jesus. Feel free to adjust the schedule to fit the time your group can spend, but remember that real discovery usually comes in discussion.

1. **5 Minutes:**   Honoring His Presence

2. **15 Minutes:** Presence Review

3. **1 hour:**   Discussion
   a. **Content Review:** What spoke to you personally...?
   b. **Clarifications:** What seemed unclear or confusing in the chapter?
   c. **Challenges:** In what ways was your life with God challenged and/or encouraged by the chapter?

4. **30 Minutes:** Reflection: What next steps seem to emerge from your reflections in this chapter?

5. **10 Minutes:** Prayer: (If only 5-10 minutes is available, break into groups of 2-3.)

Chapter1: Encounters

Personal Study and Reflection

1. How do you tend to think of God spatially? When you think of Jesus, where and in what form do you picture Him?

   Always have pictured him as one of us always walking amoungus.

2. What character did you identify with in this chapter?

   Lillian

3. In what ways did Jesus seem real to you in His appearances? What troubled you?

   Jesus meets us where we are to get our attention

4.   Review Luke 24:13-35. How does the passage speak to your life today?

Spiritual Exercise

1. **Read:** John 20:19-29, slowly and reflectively.

2. **Imagine:** Picture yourself with the disciples as Jesus appeared to them after His resurrection. Become an invisible observer. What do you notice about what hap-pens? What do you feel? What do you want to do?

3. **Listen:** Become still with God and let the Holy Spirit shed light on your experience of imagining and what you noticed and felt. What does that say about you and Jesus in your current context. Close your time by responding to Jesus in prayer.

4. **Journal:**

Group Discussion and Reflection

1. **Honoring His Presence:**   Spend several minutes of silence, becoming attentive to the reality that Jesus is present with the group. What will it mean for you to honor His Presence with you now? For example, what do you need to confess, surrender, affirm, release, etc.?

2. **Presence Review:** If Jesus were to plan to appear to you physically, how do you think He would do it in a way that would get your attention in a positive way?

3. **Discussion:**

   a. **Content Review:** What spoke to you personally in the chapter, both intellectually and emotionally?

b. **Clarifications:** What seemed unclear or confusing in the chapter?

c. **Challenges:** In what ways is your life with God challenged and/or encouraged by the chapter?

d. **Reflection:** What next steps seem to emerge from your reflections in this chapter?

e. **Prayer:** How can the group pray for you this coming week, about your relationship with God and other life issues? Take a few minutes and pray now.

Chapter 2: Close Encounters

Personal Study and Reflection

1. What would go through your mind on the way to a physical meeting with Jesus?

2. Where would you feel most comfortable meeting Jesus physically?

3. What character did you identify with in this chapter?

4. In what ways did Jesus seem real to you? What troubled you?

5. Review Matthew 6:18-22. What do you find attractive about such an invitation? What do you find frightening?

Spiritual Exercise

1. **Read:** John 4:1-13, slowly and reflectively.

2. **Imagine:** Hear Jesus speaking these familiar words to you. Pause over each word and sense how you respond to it. How would "living water" manifest itself to you in your life right now?

3. **Listen:** Become still and let the Holy Spirit reveal Jesus' personal words to you in the context of your present situation. Close your time by responding to Jesus in prayer.

4. **Journal:**

Group Discussion and Reflection

1. **Honoring His Presence:** Spend several minutes of silence, becoming attentive to the reality that Jesus is present with the group. What will it mean for you to honor His Presence with you now?

2. **Presence Review:** Review Jesus' demeanor and approach to each of the characters. Which do you feel might be most appropriate for you?

3. **Discussion:**

    a. **Content Review:** What spoke to you personally in the ways that the three characters responded to Jesus?

b. **Clarifications:** What seemed unclear or confusing in the chapter?

c. **Challenges:** In what ways is your life with God challenged and/or encouraged by the chapter?

d. **Reflection:** What next steps seem to emerge from your reflections in this chapter?

e. **Prayer:** How can the group pray for you this coming week about your relationship with God and other life issues? Take a few minutes and pray now.

Chapter 3: Discovering Love

Personal Study and Reflection

1. Where do you think Jesus would start the conversation in a physical meeting with you? conversation in a physical meeting with you?

2. What needs/issues in your life do you think He wants to address? What areas would make you feel uncomfortable?

3. What character did you identify with in this chapter?

4. In what ways did Jesus seem real to you? What troubled you?

5. Review Matthew 11:28. How does the passage speak to your life today?

Spiritual Exercise

1. **Read:** John 3:16-21, slowly and reflectively.

2. **Imagine:** Hear Jesus speaking these familiar words to you. Pause over each word and sense how you respond to it. Do you identify more with the experience of being loved by God or of being judged? Talk to Jesus about what you recognize.

3. **Listen:** Become still and let the Holy Spirit reveal Jesus' personal words to you in the context of your present situation.

4. **Journal:**

Group Discussion and Reflection

1. **Honoring His Presence:** Spend several minutes of silence, becoming attentive to the reality that Jesus is present with the group. What will it mean for you to honor His Presence with you now? For example, what do you need to confess, surrender, affirm, release, etc.?

2. **Presence Review:** How do you respond to the ways that Jesus takes charge of the meetings with each of the characters. Does this feel right or would you write His approach differently?

3. **Discussion:**

   a. **Content Review:** What spoke to you personally in the ways that the three characters responded to Jesus?

b. **Clarifications:** What seemed unclear or confusing in the chapter?

c. **Challenges:** In what ways is your life with God challenged and/or encouraged by the chapter?

d. **Reflection:** What next steps seem to emerge from your reflections in this chapter?

e. **Prayer:** How can the group pray for you this coming week about your relationship with God and other life issues? Take a few minutes and pray now.

Chapter 4: Uncomfortable Conversations

Personal Study and Reflection

1. In what ways is forgiveness an important topic of conversation between you and Jesus?

2. What challenges you about Jesus' discussion about abundant life?

3. What character did you identify with in this chapter?

4. In what ways did Jesus seem real to you? What troubled you?

5. Review John 10:1-15. What tactics is the "thief" using in your life now?

Spiritual Exercise

1. **Read:** Place yourself in the story of Like 5:17-16, as the person who was paralyzed.

2. **Imagine:** As you lay on the pallet being lowered before Jesus, become aware of the areas of paralysis that plague you. Where do you need forgiveness; where do you need abundance in your life?

5. **Listen:** Be present to Jesus and the work He wants to do in you. How is He inviting you to cooperate with His work in you? Close your time responding to Jesus in prayer, letting Him touch you with forgiveness and healing.

4. **Journal:**

Group Discussion and Reflection

1. **Honoring His Presence:** Spend several minutes of silence, becoming attentive to the reality that Jesus is present with the group. What will it mean for you to honor His Presence with you now?

2. **Presence Review:** In the story, Jesus equates "abundant life" with a "new relationship with God." In what ways do you need "newness" in your relationship with Him?

3. **Discussion:**

a. **Content Review:** What spoke to you personally in Jesus' teaching about forgiveness and abundant life?

b. **Clarifications:** What seemed unclear or confusing in the chapter?

c. **Challenges:** In what ways is your life with God challenged and/or encouraged by the chapter?

d. **Reflection:** What next steps seem to emerge from your reflections in this chapter?

e. **Prayer:** How can the group pray for you this coming week about your relationship with God and other life issues? Take a few minutes and pray now.

Chapter 5: Abundant Life

Personal Study and Reflection

1. What characteristics of abundant life would make your life "feel" abundant to you?

2. With which character's response to Jesus did you most identify?

3. In what ways did Jesus seem real to you? What troubled you?

4. Review Matthew 6:25-34. How does the passage speak to your life today?

Spiritual Exercise

1. **Read:** Place yourself in the story of Revelation 21:1-8.

2. **Imagine:** Picture the scene and feel yourself exploring and enjoying it. Compare your experience of "abundant life" in the text with your present reality. What do you find has been added and what has been left behind?

3. **Listen:** Listen to the Holy Spirit speak to you about hope. Do you find yourself reaching out for it or resisting it? Close your time responding to Jesus in prayer.

4. **Journal:**

Group Discussion and Reflection

1. **Honoring His Presence**: Spend several minutes of silence, becoming attentive to the reality that Jesus is present with the group. What will it mean for you to honor His Presence with you now? For example, what do you need to confess, surrender, affirm, release, etc.?

2. **Presence Review:** Jesus invites our three characters to live into the reality of the coming Kingdom of God and to experience its presence to the degree possible now. How does this invitation speak to your hopes and fears?

3. **Discussion:**

   a. **Content Review:** What spoke to you personally in the responses of Jim, Lillian, and Barry to Jesus' invitation to hope?

b. **Clarifications:** What seemed unclear or confusing in the chapter?

c. **Challenges:** In what ways is your life with God challenged and/or encouraged by the chapter?

d. **Reflection:** What next steps seem to emerge from your reflections in this chapter?

e. **Prayer:** How can the group pray for you this coming week about your relationship with God and other life issues? Take a few minutes and pray now.

Chapter 6: Presence Beyond

Personal Study and Reflection

1. What character did you identify with in this chapter?

2. To what extent do you embrace forgiveness and abundant life? How does that affect your relationship with others? How might the physical presence of Jesus make a difference?

3. With which character's response to Jesus did you most identify?

4. In what ways did Jesus seem real to you? What troubled you?

5. Review Philippians 1:3-11. How does it speak to your life today?

Spiritual Exercise

1. **Read:** Review the key events of your last week. Identify the things that felt joyful, painful, and/or routine. Write a key word listing of those events that stand out to you.

2. **Imagine:** Picture Jesus with you in each of the situations that you identified. Were you aware of His Presence? Do you think that He influenced the situation? If you had stopped and talked to Him about it, what might He have said?

3. **Listen:** Become still and let the Holy Spirit teach you about your experience of the Presence of Jesus with you this last week. Close your time responding to Jesus in prayer.

4. **Journal:**

Group Discussion and Reflection

1. **Honoring His Presence:** Spend several minutes of silence, becoming attentive to the reality that Jesus is present with the group. What will it mean for you to honor His Presence with you now?

2. **Presence Review:** In what ways do you discern Jesus with you in the midst of daily life? What helps remind you of His Presence?

3. **Discussion:**

   a. **Content Review:** What spoke to you personally about the ways that the three characters responded to a more experiential relationship with Jesus, be-yond their meetings with Him?

   b. **Clarifications:** To what extent did the stories of our characters seem realistic in this chapter and where did it feel fabricated?

   c. **Challenges:** In what ways is your life with God challenged and/or encouraged by the chapter?

d. **Reflection:** What next steps seem to emerge from your reflections in this chapter?

e. **Prayer:** How can the group pray for you this coming week about your relationship with God and other life issues? Take a few minutes and pray now.

Chapter 7: Discipleship

Personal Study and Reflection

1. Jesus connects a life of discipleship to the fullness of abundant life. Have you normally thought of those two subjects together or as something different?

2. Our characters felt that Jesus was asking the impossible related to His call to participate with Him in the coming of the Kingdom. How do you respond to Jesus' invitation? Do you try to get yourself "off the hook?"

3. What character did you identify with in this chapter?

4. In what ways did Jesus seem real to you? What troubled you?

5. Review Matthew 16:24-27. How does the passage speak to your life today?

Spiritual Exercise

1. **Read:** Read Ephesians 1:3-8 and Romans 8:14-17 three times slowly.

2. **Imagine:** Imagine yourself standing before the throne of God, hearing these words spoken to you by an angel or the voice of Paul. What do you notice about yourself and your feelings as you listen? What words stand out to you in the message to you?

3. **Listen:** Become still and let the Holy Spirit enlighten your experience. Let Him speak to you about your response to God's offer of forgiveness, adoption, and suffering. Close your time responding to Jesus in prayer.

4. **Journal:**

Group Discussion and Reflection

1. **Honoring His Presence:** Spend several minutes of silence, becoming attentive to the reality that Jesus is present with the group. What will it mean for you to honor His Presence with you now? For example, what do you need to confess, surrender, affirm, release, etc.?

2. **Presence Review:** How do you respond to Jesus' invitations to adoption and transformation as part of abundant life? Reflect on the Diagram in Appendix A. To what extent is your basic identity that of a son or daughter of God? Is the prospect of transformation into Christ's likeness inviting or threatening?

3. **Discussion:**

   a. **Content Review:** What spoke to you personally about Jim's interaction with Jesus about adoption and transformation?

   b. **Clarifications:** What within you competes with your calling as a child of God? In what ways can you identify your own needs for transformation?

c. **Challenges:** In what ways was your life with God challenged and/or encouraged by this chapter? Are there specific areas that you are aware of that Jesus is asking you to trust Him more in your discipleship? How can you enter in more fully into the realities of your adoption and transformation?

d. **Reflection:** What next steps seem to emerge from your reflections in this chapter?

e. **Prayer:** How can the group pray for you this coming week about your relationship with God and other life issues? Take a few minutes and pray now.

Chapter 8: Transformation

Personal Study and Reflection

1. How do you relate to the analogy Jesus' uses of the immigrant girl from India to explain our transformation into Christ-likeness?

2. What adjustments to your new home in the Kingdom of God are you experiencing and what changes still need to come?

3. How do you identify with Jesus' use of the adopted son learning to become a knight in the service of His Father?

4. Review Ephesians 6:10-13. How does the passage speak to your life today?

Spiritual Exercise

1. **Read:** Read Luke 8:26-39 three times slowly.

2. **Imagine:** Imagine yourself standing with the disciples witnessing the transformation of the Gerasene demoniac. What do you notice? How do you feel in the midst of the story and then at its conclusion? Now imagine that Jesus turns to you when you arrive on the shore and asks you to deal with the demoniac. How would you feel and respond?

3. **Listen:** Become still and let the Holy Spirit enlighten your experience. Let Him speak to about His offer of transformation in your life. Close your time responding to Jesus in prayer.

4. Journal:

Group Discussion and Reflection

1. Honoring His Presence: Spend several minutes of silence, becoming attentive to the reality that Jesus is present with the group. What will it mean for you to honor His Presence with you now? For example, what do you need to confess, surrender, affirm, release, etc.?

2. **Presence Review:** How do you respond to Jesus' invitations to transformation as part of abundant life? Reflect again on the Diagram in Appendix A. To what extent is your basic identity that of a son or daughter of God? Do you find the prospect of transformation into Christ's likeness inviting or threatening?

3. **Discussion:**

> a. **Content Review:** What spoke to you personally about Jim's interaction with Jesus about transformation?

> b. **Clarifications:** How do you respond to Jesus' analogy of the adopted young man learning to use his sword in battle? Where do you find yourself in that parable that Jesus uses?

> c. **Challenges:** In what ways was your life with God challenged and/or encouraged by this chapter?

Are there specific areas where you are aware that Jesus is asking you to trust Him more in your transformation?

d. **Reflection:** What next steps seem to emerge from your reflections in this chapter?

e. **Prayer:** How can the group pray for you this coming week about your relationship with God and other life issues? Take a few minutes and pray now.

Chapter 9: Community of Light

Personal Study and Reflection

1. What was your initial reaction to Jesus' combined meeting of our characters?

2. Do you feel that you experience Jesus more alone or in the community of others, and why?

3. What character did you identify with most in this chapter?

4. In what ways did Jesus seem real to you in the story? What troubled you?

5. Review Matthew 18: 15-35. Conclude the reading by repeating verse 20 several times. How does it speak to your life in community today?

Spiritual Exercise

1. **Read: Read** Acts 2:37-46 slowly, several times.

2. **Imagine:** See yourself as one of the people who witnessed Pentecost and became a believer following Peter's sermon. Imagine yourself forming community with the other believers in Jerusalem. What do you notice? What excites you? What threatens or worries you about life in community?

3. **Listen:** Become still and invite the Holy Spirit to speak to you about your own life of community in Christ. What tends to keep you isolated? Close your time responding to Jesus in prayer.

4. **Journal:**

Group Discussion and Reflection

1. **Honoring His Presence:** Spend several minutes of silence, becoming attentive to the reality that Jesus is present with the group. What will it mean for you to honor His Presence with you now?

2. **Presence Review:** In what ways have you become aware that Jesus is present in your group experience?

3. **Discussion:**

    a. **Content Review:** Jesus demonstrates that Christian community is built upon mutual transparency, vulnerability, and trust. Do you find these qualities easy or difficult for you and why?

    b. **Clarifications:** To what extent do you tend to look for and experience the Presence of Jesus in others?

    c. **Challenges:** What makes trusting others difficult for you?

d. **Reflection:** What next steps seem to emerge from your reflections in this chapter?

e. **Prayer:** How can the group pray for you this coming week about your relationship with God and other life issues? Take a few minutes and pray now.

CHAPTER 10: THE CHURCH

Personal Study and Reflection

1. Reflect upon your experience of church over the years, not just the one you attend now. Respond to Jesus' question about what you like and dislike? In what aspects of your church experience do you most experience the Presence of Jesus?

2. How do you respond to Jesus' allegation that most churches operate as though He is not really present—in the way the church is led, in its activities, and in its worship services? To what extent does He describe your experience?

3.   What character did you identify with in this chapter?

4.   In what ways did Jesus seem real to you? What troubled you?

5.   Review Ephesians 4:14-21. In what way does this passage challenge your life in the Church?

Spiritual Exercise

1. **Read:** Read Acts 4:32-5:16 slowly three times. Take note of the situation, the people involved, and the attributes of the church that Luke describes.

2. **Imagine:** Become a part of the story by imagining yourself as one of the characters. Maybe the Holy Spirit will guide you to become a member of the church, an elder, or possibly a visitor. What attracts you about this congregation? What worries or frightens you?

3. **Listen:** Become still in the context of your reflections about the story and let the Holy Spirit impress upon you the things that He feels are important for you in your current life. Respond to the Lord in prayer, as you feel moved.

4. **Journal:**

Group Discussion and Reflection

1. **Honoring His Presence:** Spend several minutes of silence, becoming attentive to the reality that Jesus is present with the group. What will it mean for you to honor His Presence with you now? For example, what do you need to confess, surrender, affirm, release, etc.?

2. **Presence Review:** If guests were to visit your group study, how might they discern that Jesus is actually present in the room with you?

3. **Discussion:**

   a. **Content Review:** Jesus asserts that He personally is the Leader of His Body, the Church. In what ways do you honor Him as Boss in your church and in what ways does He tend to get ignored? What would feel threatening about having Jesus physically present in the church activities of which you are a part? What would be attractive about it?

   b. **Clarifications:** If you were to canvass your un-churched community, as Jim, Lillian and Barry did, what assumptions do you think your interviewees would hold about your church?

c. **Challenges:** What would convince visitors to your church that Jesus is actually present?

d. **Reflection:** What next steps seem to emerge from your reflections in this chapter?

e. **Prayer:** How can the group pray for you this coming week about your relationship with God and other life issues? Take a few minutes and pray now.

Chapter 11: Presence Unseen

Personal Study and Reflection

1. How are you feeling about Jesus' challenge to live out His Presence in your church and community? When you picture doing that, do you imagine yourself doing things FOR Jesus, or WITH Him? Why do you think that is?

2. What helps you experience Jesus—Present with you? How do you discern His direction and leading in specific situations?

3. What character did you identify with in this chapter?

4. In what ways did Jesus seem real to you? What troubled you?

5. Review John 10:22-30. Do you feel that you hear the voice of your Shepherd's leading?

Spiritual Exercise

1. **Read:** Read Luke 6:12-19 slowly, three times.

2. **Imagine:** Imagine yourself as one of the disciples participating in the story. Observe Jesus in each movement, discerning how you might recognize the Father's Presence: -in Jesus decision to climb the mountain; -in how Jesus spent the night there; -in Jesus' selection of the apostles; -in the trip down the mountain; -in the ministry that takes place on the plain.

3. **Listen:** Let the Holy Spirit point out what He would like you to see and understand. In what ways is Jesus inviting you to serve Him in the same way that He serves the Father? Close your time responding to Jesus in prayer.

4. **Journal:**

Group Discussion and Reflection

1. **Honoring His Presence:** Spend several minutes of silence, becoming attentive to the reality that Jesus is present with the group. What will it mean for you to honor His Presence with you now?

2. **Presence Review:** In what ways do you take regular opportunities to intentionally recognize Jesus' Presence and listen to His voice?

3. **Discussion:**

   a. **Content Review:** What makes it hard for you to recognize Jesus' Presence and to discern His voice to you?

   b. **Clarifications:** How do you respond to the biblical teachings about the Holy Spirit that Jesus highlights for Barry, Lillian, and Jim? Are they passages that you have taken seriously? Why or why not?

c. **Challenges:** How do you respond to the experiential exercise that Jesus took Jim, Barry, and Lillian through to teach them how to know His Presence? How would you feel about letting the Holy Spirit teach you in the same way?

d. **Reflection:** What next steps seem to emerge from your reflections in this chapter?

e. **Prayer:** How can the group pray for you this coming week about your relationship with God and other life issues? Take a few minutes and pray now.

Chapter 12: Warriors of the Kingdom

Personal Study and Reflection

1. How did you respond to the changes that Jim, Lillian, and Barry experienced? Do they seem plausible? What caused them?

2. Review Jesus' teaching about adoption and transformation? Look again at the diagram in Appendix A. Can you identify the dynamics of that process in your own life? Have you gotten stuck? If so, where?

3. What character did you identify with in this chapter?

4. In what ways did Jesus seem real to you? What troubled you?

5. Review Ephesians 6:10-18. How does it speak to your life today?

Spiritual Exercise

1. **Read:** Reread Ephesians 6: 10-18 and have your Bible bookmarked to 1 Corinthians 13:1-13.

2. **Imagine:** Picture yourself as the warrior described in the Ephesians passage, standing with hundreds of others who have accepted the command to follow Jesus. Imagine Jesus, as He is pictured in this chapter, addressing His faithful and beloved ambassadors and speaking the words of 1 Corinthians 13:1-13. Read the Corinthians passage over several times in light in of your "full armor." How comfortable do you feel as the

adopted son or daughter of God, ready to help Him extend His love into the world? How well equipped do you feel by the transformation you have received? In what ways might you ask the Lord to transform you further?

3. **Listen:** Listen, in your heart, for how your Commander in Chief, your King, might respond to how you feel and what you need. How do you want to respond to Him? Close your time responding to Jesus in prayer.

4. **Journal:**

Group Discussion and Reflection

1. **Honoring His Presence:** Spend several minutes of silence, becoming attentive to the reality that Jesus is present with the group. What will it mean for you to honor His Presence with you now?

2. **Presence Review:** Jesus suggests that the Holy Spirit helps people come to faith as they not only hear about God's love but also see that love in action, through "miracles" performed by His followers. Can you recall the "confirmations" that have cemented your faith over the years?

3. **Discussion:**

   a. **Content Review:** How do you respond to Jesus call to function with the gifts of the Holy Spirit, in your church and in your personal life? To what extent to you feel that your life is fully surrendered to the Holy Spirit to operate through you in whatever way He chooses?

   b. **Clarifications:** How does your church background affect your ability to embrace the biblical passages discussed in this chapter? Does the perspective that Jesus proposes in the story excite or frighten you?

c. **Challenges:** In what ways do you feel challenged by Jesus statement that "religion" gets in the way of people's experience of Jesus' Presence?

d. **Reflection:** What next steps seem to emerge from your reflections in this chapter as you consider following Jesus as your King?

e. **Prayer:** How can the group pray for you this coming week about your relationship with God and other life issues? Take a few minutes and pray now. (If only 5-10 minutes is available, break into groups of 2-3.)

Chapter 13: What Now?

Personal Study and Reflection

1. How to you respond to the initial reactions of our three characters to the challenge and the following disappearance of Jesus?

2. In the story, the Holy Spirit used Barry to bring the group back from the pit of despair. What tactic has the Lord used with you over the years to redirect your focus toward Him?

3. What character did you identify with in this chapter?

4. In what ways did Jesus seem real to you? What troubled you?

5. Review Romans 8: 9-17. How does this passage speak to the role of fear in your life today?

Spiritual Exercise

1. **Read:** Read the story of raising Lazarus from the dead in John 11:1-46, with particular attention to Thomas' statement in verse 16. Jesus and His disciples had been staying away from Jerusalem because they knew that the Jewish leaders desired to kill Jesus. Now they were headed to Bethany where Jesus is to perform a miracle that will seal His death warrant.

2. **Imagine:** Let the Holy Spirit guide your imagination as you identify with one of the disciples, possibly Thomas. How do you feel about the prospective miracle vs the mortal danger ahead? What would you say to Jesus if you could?

3. **Listen:** Let the Holy Spirit show you how your situation in the biblical narrative compares to your responses to danger in your life now. What do you need from the Holy Spirit to remain true to your Lord's calling? Close your time responding to Jesus in prayer.

4. **Journal:**

Group Discussion and Reflection

1. **Honoring His Presence:** Spend several minutes of silence, becoming attentive to the reality that Jesus is present with the group. What will it mean for you to honor His Presence with you now? For example, what do you need to confess, surrender, affirm, release, etc.?

2. **Presence Review:** What frightens you about living as a follower of Jesus?

3. **Discussion:**

    a. **Content Review:** Barry, Jim, and Lillian turned to abiding prayer in the wake of their challenge and grief. How would you respond?

b. **Clarifications:** Describe your practice of prayer in which you seek to know Jesus' Presence.

c. **Challenges:** In what ways was your life with God challenged and/or encouraged by this chapter?

d. **Reflection:** What next steps seem to emerge from your reflections in this chapter?

e. **Prayer:** How can the group pray for you this coming week about your relationship with God and other life issues? Take a few minutes and pray now.

Chapter 14: Discoveries

Personal Study and Reflection

1. Reflect on the process that Barry, Jim, and Lillian used to sort out their feelings about how to follow Jesus. Do you have a trusted group that you can do that with?

2. What has Jesus been laying on your heart about participating with Him in bringing His love and Lordship to the world? What would you do if resources were not an issue and you knew you could not fail?

3. Review Mark 10:17-22. How does this passage speak to your life to-day?

Spiritual Exercise

1. **Read:** Slowly read Luke 10:1-20, several times.

2. **Imagine:** Let the Holy Spirit guide your imagination as you identify with one of the disciples. What do you notice in the situation? What do you feel as one of the seventy disciples being sent out and as one of the ones returning to Jesus?

3. **Listen:** Spend time in silence, reflecting on your responses. What do you discover about yourself? What does Jesus want to say to you in your current situation and life now? Close your time responding to Jesus in prayer.

4. **Journal:**

Group Discussion and Reflection

1. **Honoring His Presence:** Spend several minutes of silence, becoming attentive to the reality that Jesus is present with the group. What will it mean for you to honor His Presence with you now?

2. **Presence Review:** What are you discovering about your own life with Jesus actually Present with you?

3. **Discussion:**

   a. **Content Review:** What spoke to you personally about Jim's, Lillian's, and Barry's dreams and visions?

b. **Clarifications:** What seemed unclear or confusing in this chapter?

c. **Challenges:** In what ways is your life with God challenged and/or encouraged by this chapter?

d. **Reflection:** What next steps seem to emerge from your reflections in this chapter?

e. **Prayer:** How can the group pray for you this coming week about your relationship with God and other life issues? Take a few minutes and pray now.

Chapter 15: Presence Unfolding

Personal Study and Reflection

1. How did you respond to the events and outcomes in this chapter?

2. What felt real and plausible and what questions were raised?

3. Which of the three characters and their ventures could you identify with? How might Jesus be calling you to join Him in your "town of Emmaus?"

4. Review John 14:12-15. How does it speak to your life today?

Spiritual Exercise

1. **Read:** Slowly read John 14:16-21 several times.

2. **Imagine:** Picture yourself sitting with Jesus today. Where would you like to meet with Him? Listen to Jesus speaking these words to you. Notice which parts of His message excites you and which parts cause you pause or concern? How might Jesus leave this place with you as He invites you to ponder His words?

3. **Listen:** Be still and become an observer to your own heart. Look for Jesus' specific invitation to you. When He said, "Get up, let us go from this place." what might that mean for you now?

4. **Journal:**

Group Discussion and Reflection

1. **Honoring His Presence:** Spend several minutes of silence, becoming attentive to the reality that Jesus is present with the group. What will it mean for you to honor His Presence with you now?

2. **Presence Review:** Which of the three stories in this chapter caught your attention and imagination?

3. **Discussion:**

   a. **Content Review:** What spoke to you personally about what you would like to see God do in your life in the next ten years? In the next month?

b. **Clarifications:** What questions emerged for you in reading this concluding chapter and how are those questions important for your ongoing walk with Jesus?

c. **Challenges:** In what ways was your life with God challenged and/or encouraged by this chapter?

d. **Reflection:** How did you respond to the ending of the story? What next steps seem to emerge from your reflections in this chapter?

e. **Prayer:** How can the group pray for you this coming week about your relationship with God and other life issues? Take a few minutes and pray now.

4. Discuss the Follow-up Retreat

Appendix A: Abundant Life

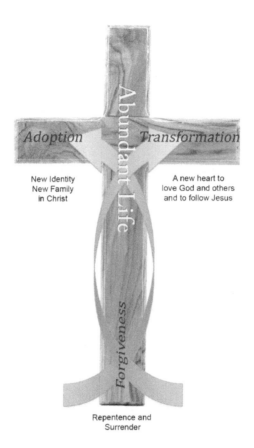

Graphic by Roy Graham, OIC

Appendix B: Retreat Outlines

My monk mentor once told me, "Sometimes we have to get off the scene to give ourselves space to become attentive to God." Presence was conceived to entice people to long for a personal, living, relationship with Jesus Christ, and through Him, God the Father, all wrapped up in the swirling life of the Holy Spirit. Like Jim, Lillian, and Barry, we can get so caught up in daily life that we miss the words, the heart impressions, the glimpses of God's Presence. We simply don't notice, or if we do, we tuck them back in our minds intending to return to them later, but forget. So, I suggest that you do something different.

When we close the office door, put down the cell phone and computer, leave behind the traffic and the responsibilities and go to a quiet place and become still, an amazing thing can happen – we begin to notice! And when we notice and ponder and listen, our moment can become a profound experience of Jesus – Present. He has used "off the scene" places profoundly in my personal journey with Him, so I'd like to encourage them for you and your group.

The following retreat outlines can be used by individuals or groups. However, when we go away "together" with Jesus, we often experience Him more profoundly, depending on how we structure our time.

I offer two retreat outlines, one that can be used BEFORE the study group, and the other could be used AFTER.

The first outline might be used for an **Introductory Retreat**. As we saw with Lillian, Barry, and Jim, their experience of Jesus significantly increased as they came together and learned to know and trust each other. So, an introductory retreat for you and your group, <u>done before you begin the study</u>, could deepen and significantly cement the entire ongoing process you've been through in *Discovering Christ's Presence.*

The **Follow-up Retreat** can then be used to unpack the overall small group experience of reading and reflecting on *Presence.* Strangely, even weekly discussions and profound encounters with the Lord can soon get lost or submerged under the pressures of "normal" life. During the discussions, we long for a "new normal," but we can soon lose track of the Lord's invitation. In a follow-up retreat, you can review what the Lord has said to you over the previous months and gain a clearer picture of what life with Jesus, experientially Present, might be like and what you can do to co-operate with that reality.

First, some suggestions for both retreats:

Location: Quiet, comfortable, undistracting, beautiful, places to be together and alone.

Time: Enough time to relax and decompress; the more the better. It takes time to rest and focus before we can really begin to give space for God and one another – one day including travel just won't cut it. Having said that, we all know that time is our most precious commodity. So, one has to measure the capacity of the group. I would suggest two full days, exclusive of travel. For example, travel on Thursday afternoon or evening; spend all day Friday and Saturday; eat, worship, and discuss on Sunday morning, and then leave for home after lunch. However, you can make it work, adjust the suggested modules below to fit your needs. Remember, though, that personal time and group time provide the "spaces" when God's Presence can best be discerned. So, if possible, leave off the volley ball game, talent show, or shopping trip to the nearby town. Just BE together with Jesus.

Note: I have not indicated the amount of time to be spent in each module. The retreat coordinator will want to be sensitive to the group size and the amount of time it takes to accomplish each module. While there needs to be some amount of unstructured "free time," the retreat outlines provide a significant amount of personal time. Participants sacrificed hard earned money and precious time for these experiences and deserve more than a getaway rest that they could do on their own. So fit the time frames to fit your group.

Along another line, I have not provided modules to talk about the church specifically. While Jesus' challenge to the church in *Presence* is significant, it can also be easy for participants to avoid personal encounter by focusing on what's wrong with the church or how we should fix this or that— outside themselves. Church transformation comes through the personal transformation of its members. So, while discussion of the church should not be made taboo, the leader will want to continually redirect discussion to the lives of the participants when necessary. For Solitude times and for walks in two's, it might be helpful to provide copies of the reflection questions and guidelines for participants to take along, to help them stay on track.

Introductory Retreat

Preparation:

1. If possible read *Presence* before you come.

2. A week or two prior, ask several people of faith to pray for you, your family, your preparation, travel, and your time with God. Many "shields of faith" will provide the spiritual space for you to enjoy the physical space of the retreat as well as protect your family, friends and co-workers.

3. Spend an intentional hour or so surrendering yourself and the people and tasks within your care to God. In the context of His forgiveness and love, share with Him your concerns and fears. Be specific in asking for what you sense you need to happen in your coming time away. Commit to Him to be as honest, open, and vulnerable as you can, and to seek out at least one other person to get to know better.

4. Leave at home options for an alternative to Jesus and your group, such as books, radios, CD players, computers, etc. Most of us HAVE to have our cell phones with us (what if the world needed us super-heroes?), but commit to emergency use only.

5. Relax and let Jesus lead.

Retreat Modules:

Worship
Solitude
Rest
Guided reflection
Sharing
Prayer, and of course,
Food

Over a two-day and three evening retreat, rotate through these modules several times. For example:

First Evening:

Food and Fellowship

Spend half an hour or so sharing snacks or dinner, inviting each person to share with the whole group who they are and what they hope to receive from the retreat. Nothing worse than feeling isolated in a group of people one really doesn't know. If there are many people who don't know one another, use name tags.

Worship

A word about worship: Worship should attempt to model the listening posture of the retreat. Music and singing proves really helpful for most of us. Try to pick songs that address God personally, avoiding songs with language that projects God as somewhere other than present. Use short periods of silence between songs, again modeling that we expect God to respond to us when we communicate with Him. Include Scripture readings that can help set the stage for a time on the mountain with Jesus, again leaving silent spaces after the readings so that participants can become attentive and listen. Invite prayers from the group.

Solitude.

Invite Participants to spend the rest of the evening alone, resting, praying, walking, sleeping, etc. Ask them to keep silence until breakfast the next morning to the extent possible. Jesus just might want to be alone with them.

First Full Day Morning:

Food and Fellowship

Worship

Spiritual Exercise:

Choose a Spiritual Exercise in one of the early chapters of *Discovering Christ's Presence*, giving participants about half an hour to work through it alone.

Sharing Spiritual History.

1. Prepare a spiritual history timeline, marking significant events, relationships, difficulties, realizations, etc. Start from birth to the present. Take one hour. (An easy way to do this is with sticky notes that can be pasted and rearranged on an 11/14 poster board, chronologically.

2. Share the timeline in groups of 2's or 3's.
Emphasize the importance of sharing at a level where
one feels comfortable, with confidentiality, good
listening, no judgment, fixing, or advice. Take about
half an hour for each person to share. Make sure
everyone has an opportunity to share. Close each
sharing with prayer for that person, thanking God that
by His Lordship and presence in each event (known or
unknown) the story has become sacred ground.

Free time followed by Food and Fellowship

Afternoon:

Solitude:

Call the group together for instructions before they
disperse. Invite participants to reflect personally on
their own history with God described in the timeline.
People may find this easiest on a walk alone, sitting in
a beautiful spot, or in their room. What patterns do
they see? How has their view of God changed over the
years? If Jesus were to appear to them physically in the
solitude time, what do they think He would want to
talk about relative to their history with Him?
Encourage them not to sabotage another person's time
with God by engaging in conversation. Given the
amount of time available, invite participants to take a
nap before the next session.

Discovering Longing

Reflection: Every one of us longs for more in our relationship with God, whether we know it or not. God has placed the "desires of our hearts" within us for deeper intimacy with Him. This longing may be experienced by many of us negatively, as aspects of our relationship with God and church that we don't like. In this session, invite participants to try to put words to that longing for relationship in a positive way. The Longing here is to be about our personal relationship with God, not about how we serve Him. Often a picture or metaphor can prove helpful in articulating a reality that is really deeper than words. Here are some steps that may prove helpful:

1. Have someone, who has thought through his/her own longing, share her/his hunger for God and what its realization would mean for them personally.

2. Give participants an opportunity to take an hour or so alone to review their timeline and look for the longings that were present at each stage of their journey. Each person should also ask the Holy Spirit to bring to mind a favorite Scripture passage, a picture, or a metaphor that might embody or symbolize the longing for a wonderful relationship with God now. Ask them to write out their Longing Statements, in a page or less.

3. Divide into twos or threes and spend about half an hour each, sharing longings, ending in prayer asking God to lead them into its reality.

Free Time followed by Supper.

Evening:

Worship

Sharing: If the group is large, divide into smaller groups of 4 or so for sharing. Invite each person to share about the discoveries of the day. Remind them that this is not about "success" stories, but about the ways they felt that they encountered Jesus as Present. It is a good opportunity to remind participants that this is a time for listening. While one could ask clarifying questions, advice-giving or problem-solving is not appropriate. Close the time of sharing with prayer relative to the things shared and needs expressed.

Food and Fellowship

Second Full Day

Food (Breakfast) and Fellowship

Worship

Spiritual Exercise:

Choose a Spiritual Exercise in one of the early chapters of the Study Guide, giving participants about half an hour working through it alone.

Discovery Walk:

Divide the group to two's (use one three if necessary). The twos should not be the same ones that shared their timelines together the previous day, if possible. To the extent that the retreat place, weather, etc., allow, ask the twos to go for a walk for an hour. Give them an extra 15 minutes to get ready before and to regroup after. Walks should be planned to make discussion easy in an atmosphere of privacy and lack of distraction. A vigorous climb to the nearest peak or a stroll through a shopping mall might not prove helpful, for example. Invite the participants to reflect together on the following questions. Suggest that one person share on one question, then the other share on the same question, and so on.

1.   Thinking through the spiritual timeline developed yesterday, how has Jesus made His Presence known over the years and what environments have helped make that possible? For example: in times of solitude or with others? In nature or in cities? In Scripture reading and study? In worship in church? Etc. To what extent are you intentionally seeking the Lord in the environments where He has traditionally met you?

2.   Share an overview of the Longing Statement you developed the day before. As you imagine Jesus fulfilling that Longing, what do you find really

exciting and attractive and what do you find
frightening, threatening, or worrisome? What in
you might tend to block or avoid Jesus' attempts to
reveal His Presence and deepen your relation-ship
with Him?

Free time followed by Food (Lunch) and Fellowship

Afternoon:

Solitude:

Invite participants to reflect personally about their
morning walk discussion. Ask the Lord to reveal more
about what keeps them from seeking the Lord in the
places where He seems to rendezvous with them. What
frightens them about the implications of a deeper
relationship with God? Where in their own history do
they find the roots of those fears? How are those fears
reflected in their relationships with others? Encourage
them to pick a place for reflection that will avoid a nap.

Group Discussion:

Divide the participants into groups of three (one group
of four if necessary). To the extent possible, have the
groups made up of participants that have not be in the
same group before. Invite each person to share their
discoveries of the morning solitude time. Where do

they find resistances to greater intimacy with God, and to what extent do they know where those resistances come from in their own history? After each person has had an opportunity to share, invite the participants to spend time in prayer together, surrendering the resistances they have discovered and opening their hearts to greater degrees of receptivity.

Free Time followed by Supper.

Evening:

Worship

Personal Reflection:

Staying in the room, invite participants to engage in a personal, Holy Spirit guided, reflection. Have them imagine Jesus appearing to them in physical form. Picture it. What place would Jesus choose? How would He get your attention? What would He say? How would you respond? What topic would Jesus pick for your next meeting? What feelings emerge in you during the process, and what do they tell you?

Sharing:

If the group is large, divide into smaller groups of 4 or so for sharing. Invite each person to share about the Discoveries of the day. Close the time of sharing with prayer relative to the things shared and needs expressed.

Food and Fellowship

Third Partial Day

Food (Breakfast) and Fellowship

Worship

Spiritual Exercise:

> Choose another spiritual exercise, from the chapters above, giving participants about half an hour working through it alone.

Solitude:

> Invite participants to spend the next hour alone with God. Give them permission to stay in the meeting room, go for a walk, return to their room, etc. However, encourage them not to sabotage another person's time with God by engaging in conversation. During the hour, people should attempt to become attentive to Jesus as Present with them. They might consider opening the time by verbalizing the concerns on their hearts, but then becoming silent and simply attentive. Those who like to journal may do so to capture and summarize their thoughts and experiences, but should not spend the whole time journaling

Group Discussion:

Invite the whole group to process their experiences, both of connection with Jesus and of frustration. Were they able to connect with their longing and did it prove helpful in focusing their attempts to become attentive to the Presence of Jesus? What did they discover got in their way in trying to discern the Presence of Jesus? How might they ask the Holy Spirit to help them in their ongoing reading, reflection, and group discussions in the coming months? Close the discussion time and the retreat with prayer for the help need-ed.

Food and Fellowship and Departure

Follow-up Retreat

The purpose of the Follow-up Retreat is to help participants process what they have discovered during the small group meetings. It will be important to identify some of the next steps for cooperating with Jesus in deepening intimacy and participation. Some participants, maybe most, will have discovered that the study unearthed more questions that it gave answers. Participants may have expected that small group interaction would build a nice box for our experience of Jesus as Present and tie a pretty bow on top. We find, however, that not only is God more mysterious than we thought, but we are far more complex than we could have guessed. We find that Jesus does not reveal Himself as predictably as we would like. Worse, we also discover that we are all filled with mixed motives and desires. A "Jesus up in the sky" may have felt much safer; Jesus in my face can really become threatening.

The process of the Follow-up Retreat should reflect the elements described in Presence to the extent possible:

1. Personal encounter with Jesus
2. Personal reflection and discernment
3. Group encounter with Jesus
4. Group reflection and discernment.

Therefore, the retreat is designed to mirror the major movements of the *Presence* story, with opportunity for participants to capture some of their key discoveries and to chart a way forward. It is important, to the extent possible, for every member of the study group to be present. The Lord has used the dynamics of the small group study process to build the participants into a community where love, forgiveness, and mutual discernment have created a safe place for ongoing discovery.

Review the guidelines and desired atmosphere for the Introductory Retreat, as they also apply here. The following retreat outline is designed for two full days, but can be adapted to fit the time available. Hopefully, this retreat can be more participative and interactive than the first one. Invite particular participants to lead various modules, using their own story in that area as a short introduction. No one should be forced or coerced, but encouraged that they have something special to offer. Let the people you pick go through the retreat outline and pick the modules they would like to lead. Leadership would include getting the group together at the appropriate time and starting on time; introducing the topic with a personal story; providing the instructions for that module; watching the clock to help the process stay on time.

Preparation:

1.   Review your notes from your *Discovering Christ's Presence* study guide and mark discoveries that you feel, in retrospect, proved significant. Be sure to note answers to question 3.d (Reflection on Next Steps) in each chapter.

2.   A week or two prior, ask several people of faith to pray for you, for your preparation, travel, and your time with God. Many "shields of faith" will provide the spiritual space for you to enjoy the physical space of the retreat as well as protect your family, friends and co-workers.

3. Spend an intentional hour or so surrendering yourself and the people and tasks within your care to God. In the context of His forgiveness and love, share with Him your concerns and fears. Be specific in asking for what you sense you need to happen in your coming time away. Commit to Him to be as honest, open, and vulnerable as you can, and to seek out at least one other person to get to know better.

4. Leave home options for an "alternative to Jesus and your group," such as books, radios, CD players, computers, etc. Most of us HAVE to have our cell phones with us (what if the world needed us super-heroes?), but commit to emergency use only.

5. Relax and let Jesus lead.

Retreat Modules:

Worship
Solitude
Rest
Guided reflection
Sharing
Prayer, and of course
Food.

Over a two-day and three evening retreat, rotate through these modules several times. For example:

First Evening:

Food and Fellowship.

Spend half an hour or so sharing snacks or dinner, inviting each person to share with the whole group what they hope to receive from the retreat.

Worship.

A word, again, about worship. Worship should attempt to model the listening posture of the retreat. Music and singing proves really helpful for most of us. Try to pick songs that address God personally, avoiding songs with language that projects God as somewhere other than present. Use short periods of silence between songs, again modeling that we expect God to respond to us when we communicate with Him. Include Scripture readings that can help set the stage for a time on the mountain with Jesus, again leaving silent spaces after the readings so that participants can become attentive and listen. Invite prayers from the group.

Solitude.

Invite Participants to spend the rest of the evening alone, resting, praying, walking, sleeping, etc. Ask them to keep silence until breakfast the next morning to the extent possible.

First Full Day Morning:

Food and Fellowship

Worship

Follow-up Retreat

Spiritual Exercise:

Have the module leader guide the group through one of the Exercises from the Study Guide that he or she felt personally significant.

Solitude and Personal Reflection:

Review the Study Review that you did in preparation for the retreat. What consistent themes seem to emerge, both in your personal reading and in your reflections on the group discussion time? What do you feel that God accomplished in you during the ongoing group process? What do you wish He had accomplished but didn't appear to?

Group Sharing:

Share in the whole group the insights you received in your Personal Reflection above. This is a time for listening, not commenting or problem solving. After the sharing, invite the group to record common themes that seemed to emerge. Explain that they will want to be attentive to how the Lord will address those themes in the coming hours of the retreat.

Free time followed by Food and Fellowship

Afternoon:

Solitude:

Invite participants to find a quiet place where they can focus on Jesus, Present to them, and spend about an hour. It might be helpful to take the Presence book and the study guide. Reflect on Jesus' appearances to the characters in the story and the unique ways He appeared and dealt with each one of them. Which of the ways Jesus connected in His ongoing individual conversations did you most identify with? Imagine yourself in that scene and ask Jesus to make Himself known to you in the way He knows is best for the moment. Recall the ways Jesus taught the three characters to identify His Presence in Chapter 9. Practice with Jesus in your imagination with attentiveness to your own heart. Become still and be with Jesus for the purpose of loving Him rather than for what you might be able to get from Him. Journal your time.

Group Communion with the Trinity:

Have the participants join together, sitting in a circle. The purpose of this time will be to commune with Jesus as a group through speaking to Him, listening attentively, speaking insights, and worship. Place three empty chairs together in the group, one a rocking chair if available.

Follow-up Retreat

1. Silence: Invite participants to reflect on their time with Jesus earlier in the afternoon and what they experienced or didn't experience. In the silence, focus on the Presence of Jesus and, in Him, the Father and the Holy Spirit.

2. Invite each person, as they feel comfortable, to verbalize what they would like to say to the Trinity, first in the category of praise and thanksgiving, then repentance and forgiveness, then questions and requests. The leader can monitor the time and activity, and lead the transition from topic to topic. Follow this section with at least three minutes of silence.

3. Invite those who would like, to speak out loud to the Lord indicating what they think they may have sensed or heard during the prayer time, either for themselves or for the group. Where others have sensed the same message, they may speak out in confirmation. Allow spaces for silence between sharing, and be careful not to close the time prematurely. Close this time when everyone has finished with another three minutes of silence. During this time, participants can journal key words to help them recall insights they felt were significant.

4. The leader should choose two or three choruses or a hymn that expresses love and devotion to God, one that is well known to the participants, for them to sing in closing worship.

Free Time followed by Supper

Follow-up Retreat

Worship

Debrief:

In the whole group, debrief the experiences of the day. What proved helpful in discerning the Lord? What did people discover? What implications for their own lives do they sense? This is a time for sharing, discussion, and exploration, not problem solving. Expect and allow people to have different experiences and perspectives, trusting Jesus to shepherd each one appropriately.

Holy Communion:

Share Holy Communion together in a manner that best fits the participants in the group, and intentionally recognizes Jesus as Present in and with the group.

Food and Fellowship

Second Full Day

Food (Breakfast) and Fellowship

Worship

Follow-up Retreat

Spiritual Exercise:

Choose a Spiritual Exercise that proved particularly meaningful to the person leading this session. Give at least a half hour for the Exercise.

Solitude:

Invite the participants to find a quiet place, either in the facility or on a walk alone. Reflect on the explorations that the Lillian, Jim, and Barry made in the town of Emmaus and the attitudes that people had about Jesus and the church. Spend some time reflecting about people in your environment (family, friends, co-workers, etc.). In what ways do you see Jesus hidden from people by the ways that Christians live out their relationship with God? Jesus challenged our characters to let Him be seen in their lives, but received a pretty strong push back from each. What push-backs do you feel in your own heart to Jesus' call to live out His Presence to those who don't yet know Him? Our characters discovered that their own needs for such things as security, self-esteem, comfort, control, etc. took precedence over Jesus' call to disciple-ship. What needs do you have that keeps you from fully embracing Jesus' love for others?

Discovery Walk:

Divide the group to two's, inviting them to debrief their pervious interactions with Jesus and their own hearts in their time of solitude, closing their time in prayer for one another.

Food (Lunch) and Fellowship

Afternoon:

Solitude:

Take an hour alone (in a fashion what will prevent a nap) and reflect on the chart in Appendix A which summarize the process of abundant life that Jesus taught in our story. In light of what you have discovered about yourself over the years and in the course of this group study, identify where Jesus might be teaching, or wanting to teach you about each of the processes He describes:

1. Forgiveness

2. Repentance and Surrender

3. Adoption into His family, gaining His family identity and shedding that of the world

4. Transformation as the Holy Spirit remakes us into the image of Christ so that we can love God and others and learn to follow Jesus in the power of the Holy Spirit

Ask the Holy Spirit to give you insight. Journal your reflections in each category.

Food and Fellowship

Follow-up Retreat

Small Group Debriefing:

Divide the participants into groups of three or four. Invite them to share the discoveries in the previous exercise. After each person has had an opportunity to share, pray for each person in the group, surrendering blocks that have been identified and asking the Holy Spirit to continue the process of producing abundant life in the ways that person has identified needing.

Free Time followed by Food (Supper) and Fellowship

Worship

Whole Group Debrief:

Review the themes that were recorded from the Group Discussion on the first full morning. Invite participants to share what they have discovered during the day's events. What has God revealed? What questions have emerged? After the sharing, the leader should note the time available and give a certain amount of time for each person to share. If time remains, members of the group may ask clarifying questions or respond in some way. Again, invite the group to complete the discussion by noting common themes.

Holy Communion

Food and Fellowship

Third Day Morning

Morning Prayer before Breakfast:

Invite participants to prepare for this session the evening before. Each one should pick something to share in the group as part of Morning Prayer worship. They can select a Scripture reading, a hymn, a poem, an entry from their journal, a paragraph from Presence, a piece of art or an object, and so on. Each offering should be about a minute or less. The leader should form the whole group in a circle and begin the time with an opening prayer. The Morning Prayer should then proceed as the participants offer, as prayer, what they have brought by reading it aloud, showing it, etc. (Avoid handing out material.) Rather than going around the circle, invite each one to share when they feel it is appropriate, but try not to leave too much silence between offerings. Instruct the group to try to keep the process moving. Close the Morning Prayer by praying the Lord's Prayer together.

Food (Breakfast) and Fellowship

Worship

Follow-up Retreat

Spiritual Exercise:

Repeat the Spiritual Exercise in Chapter 15. Do it afresh rather than referring to your journal from the Study Group. The Exercise is repeated here for convenience.

1. **Read:** Slowly read John 14:16-21 several times.

2. **Imagine:** Picture yourself sitting with Jesus today. Where would you like to meet with Him? Listen to Jesus speaking these words to you. Notice which parts of His message excites you and which parts cause you pause or concern? How might Jesus leave this place with you as He invites you to ponder His words?

3. **Listen:** Be still and become an observer to your own heart. Look for Jesus' specific invitation to you. When He said, "Get up, let us go from this place." what might that mean for you now?

4. **Journal:**

Solitude:

Recall the last chapter of Presence and the changes that evolved in our three characters, in their church, and their town. Ask the Holy Spirit to help you "dream dreams and see visions," and reflect on the changes you would like to see 1) in your own life, 2) in your church, particularly your personal involvement, and 3) in your "town," the people around you, as they relate to you. After asking the Holy Spirit, become still and attentive. Let the images come as they will, and don't try to force some order on them. After the "ideas" stop coming, remain still and just sit with the Lord. How do you feel about what you have "seen?" What do those feelings tell you? Let Jesus lead. Journal a few key words that capture what happened.

Debrief in Two's:

Share what happened in your Spiritual Exercise and Solitude time. Pray for one another in the way that feels appropriate.

Whole Group Discussion:

In the whole group, invite participants to answer the following question: "In light of your knowledge and experience of Jesus' Presence with you all the time, what new thing would you do in the years ahead, if you knew you couldn't fail?" Give the participants a few minutes to consider the question and then invite their responses as they feel ready to share.

Food (Lunch) and Fellowship and Departure

.

Interact with the author and others reading *Presence*

Find out how others are using *Presence* and this study guide, *Discovering Christ's Presence*, and dialogue about your own journey with Jesus—Present. Go to Tom's publishing website. Find new resources as they are developed with links to others being used by God in the world wide movement of God's call to growing intimacy with God through the experience of Jesus—Present. See: www.TomAshbrook.com

Spiritual Formation Resource for Individuals, Spiritual Directors, and Congregations

By R. Thomas Ashbrook

Mansions of the Heart: Exploring the Seven Stages of Spiritual Growth, uses Teresa of Avila's seven mansions to explore the life-long journey of spiritual growth. While *Mansions* has been used with great success by seminaries, spiritual formation programs, and Christian leaders, the *Mansions Study Guide,* by Tom Ashbrook and Ted Wueste now makes *Mansions* accessible to small groups and spiritual direction relationships. This interactive study for personal reflection and group discussion enables Jesus followers to discover where they are in their journey of spiritual growth and learn how to cooperate with the Holy Spirit's transformation work.

See www.mansionsoftheheart.com for ordering information and discounts.

CRM EMPOWERING LEADERS

CRM (Church Resource Ministries: www.crmleaders.org) is a movement committed to developing leaders to strengthen and multiply the Church worldwide.

More than three hundred and fifty CRM missionaries live and minister in nations on every continent, coaching, mentoring, and apprenticing those called to lead the Christian movement in their settings. This results in the multiplication of godly leaders who have a passion for their work and who are empowered to multiply their lives and ministry. Through them, CRM stimulates movements of fresh, authentic churches, holistic in nature, so that the name of God is renowned among the nations. See www.crmleaders.org. Tom Ashbrook serves with CRM as the leader of the Order of *Imago Christi*. See www.crmleaders.org.

The Order of *Imago Christi* forms CRM's spiritual formation

ministry to Christian leaders around the world. At *Imago Christi's* core lies a covenant community that develops spiritual formation resources and coaches leaders and churches to be able to live and lead with a spiritual authority grounded in loving intimacy with Jesus. Tom Ashbrook founded Imago Christi and plays an integral part in this community.

See www.ImagoChristi.org.